MICHAEL KRÜGER

SEASONAL TIME CHANGE

SELECTED POEMS

Translated by Joseph Given

LONDON NEW YORK CALCUTTA

 **GOETHE**
INSTITUT

This application was supported by a grant from
the Goethe Institut, India.

Seagull Books, 2021

Originally published as *Umstellung der Zeit. Gedichte*
by Michael Krüger © Suhrkamp Verlag, Berlin, 2013

First published in English translation by Seagull Books, 2015
English translation © Joseph Given, 2015

ISBN 978 0 8574 2 827 1

British Library Cataloguing-in-Publication Data
A catalogue record for this book is available from the British Library

Typeset by Seagull Books, Calcutta, India
Printed and bound by WordsWorth India, New Delhi, India

CONTENTS

I

II

IV

I

'Reason always dresses for mourning.'

Ramón Gómez de la Serna

My Desk in Allmanshausen

In the house beside mine, just up the hill,
lived Mussolini's foreign minister
before he was captured and taken to Italy and
 hanged.
And one further on was Hitler's favourite poet,
Hanns Johst, whose words were obviously
 inspired here.
I look at cows, squirrels and horses;
at the open window I hear the distant Autobahn.
No one's forcing anyone
to accuse humanity of doing good.
Once the sun goes down, there's me
in the window; of course, mirrors can also be
 wrong.

Not a Haiku

Before my window
a dead blackbird.
I wait for an hour
on the seasonal
time change.

Postcard, May 2012 *

The terrace door is open and
dandelions, those common yellow guerrillas,
are sweeping relentlessly over the lawn;
the squirrel's looking for
last year's nuts. Rain's expected;
the swing is dreaming of wind already.
If the fat Sunday papers
are right, none of all that exists—
neither the thrush nor the elegy
it entrusts to the maple nor
the weeds, friends of the bees.
Because of our scorn for imperfection
an invisible machine is now working
towards perfection. By the way,
the apple tree, which, like me,
first saw the light of the world in wartime,
is starting to bloom again too.

Three Winds, Pentecost

A scallywag of wind
sways in the curtains;
another reads my book
in mad haste;
a third gathers up stones,
so the world won't
get lost before its time.
Which language
do we have to speak,
to help the world to heal?
And are there really
fifty words for light?

May

It is May and I'm reading
in one of the uncut books
that my life has already been written,
year for year. On the last page
I read the way my life should have been
but wasn't.
A reliable source, easily edited.
The merciful author tries to persuade me
not to finish it off; love's lost labours.
In the evening, I see myself in the window,
astonishment personified, as if
I had no other choice, the book before me,
heavy dark slab of granite.

Near Münsing *

I walked towards Münsing on the forest path.
Tin percussion instruments were playing,
as if a dwarfs' orchestra was hiding there.
It takes time to really understand—
the trees will outlive you
whilst the butterfly, despite its beauty, won't.
Shoes crackling underfoot. Rain,
and hope comes and goes with it.
Have I taken a wrong turn? It's no cause for
    shame
to no longer know which path you took.
A word occurs to me—lupins.
It leads me back to my childhood,
to a time before the invention of shame.
I hope the trees don't notice!

Long Conversation

with the sycamore in my garden.
Five trunks from one root,
a stuttering shadow
when the birds depart.

I will outlive you;
just a remark,
perhaps a simple way of
not betraying what the truth is.

Five gods,
unified at the root,
but above just idle chatter
when discussion is sought.

Crow-Eater

Crows, tells one
who survived the war,
have to be cooked
with the wood of the pine,
to bind the poisons,
and served with sorrel
which animals spurn.
The order of a world at peace
is hard to understand.
Here we sit in the open air
and marvel at the sunset.
The crows on the pine
will have the final word.

I Cannot Divine What it Meaneth *

In the wood I found raspberries,
tightly wound with lamellar, striped ivy,
that hugged ruins, a crumbly wall
on which a bell hung. It was hot from the sun.
Just for a laugh I pressed the button of the bell.
Then a couple of gods started walking across the
      glade
with light steps, engrossed in talk,
and behind them another one; he wanted to be
      alone.
The things gods talk about. If it's at all true,
we'll soon be aware of the exact date of our
      deaths,
I heard one say, it's all already written.
I'd understood; I didn't want to realize.

Wooden House *

for Alfred Kolleritsch

You have to stand with your back
to the wall in the evening light.
Then you'll see the storm
announcing its arrival in the crown
of the lime. The mad blackbirds,
as if from some late work.
We will be judged on the number
of times we withheld the truth
although the word lay warm on the tongue.
A glance at the hastening clouds,
and you understand the gulf
between the heavens and the earthly world.
Your back to the warm wood,
then the sunset.

Happiness

Like the scent of lupins
or milfoil after the rain,
the knotgrass that the stone
won't surrender.
It takes too long
before you get sent back
to childhood,
when the words still had time
to reveal their richness.
A late realization
won through weakness.
If you showed me
a broad bean now,
I would fall down dead
with happiness.

Walk in the Woods

No one has ever described the sweet smell of cut
    wood
in such a way that we could do without it; or
indeed, hardly anyone at least, the moment of
    silence
when the birds collapse into their frightful
slumber and
the grumbling of the pines sounds like
the far-off echo of disaster
running freely through the world
in search of a new name.
In other parts of the world, people ask themselves
if we created the world or whether it was perhaps
created for us and by whom.
Here, nobody asks. Every stone is convinced
that its rightful place is the one that it occupies,
and the tattered hedge, which grew infinitely
    slowly,
there in the clearing, wants to know nothing
of the laws of nature. Here it stands

at its own risk. If you stand long enough
beside it, you can hear the birds breathing.
Soon they're gone. It's still not clear
whether they fly to Athens or Jerusalem
because if you belong to the forest,
you forget where home is.
Bing Bang—Bing Bang—yet again
the church bell attempts to report a fire
that can't be extinguished.

A Friend

He is fascinated
by grasses,
knows everything
about oat grass
and bent awn
and dogstail.
One-sided inflorescence.
Even cocksfoot,
with its knotted spikelets,
is familiar to him.

But he knows nothing
of bittercress,
ox-eye or hogweed,
yellow rattle or meadowsweet.
To him they seem
like unencrypted blunders.

In the field he counts clouds;
he keeps away from novels.

Sometimes I see him
whispering to the red bent grass
to tame his mourning.

Twilight

Now you can see the fine rips
in the shadow; and there,
where the stream burrows into the lake,
so that it froths brown,
the day loses its light mood.
And the wind sinks its claws
into the pale branches of the birches,
hands over its gift.
Ach, the joyful *and* which binds
all without complaint.
Now you can see the path
that leads into the village lighting up.
Farewell lurks in every footprint.
You have to get in line,
into the queue of pebbles at the lakeside,
for the sake of a higher justice.
A last ship sails past;
on board, hits are being sung
about a love that never ends.
The world has become so very small

that low-flying swallows
devour it in passing.

The Last Day of August

The apple tree, straining under
its load, will soon be casting
its fruit onto the grass,
because I didn't pluck it.
The wind is calm and yet
a single leaf begins
to spin madly.
Something isn't right.
Even the birds shut their beaks.
Something we called the density of life,
after long brooding,
now questions the Word.
Language fails.
The density is mute;
and there's the apple, never far from the tree.

The Death of the Birch, 2011

First it was fungus growing
out of its hip, fat sponge,
then the wind took its leaves
and let it fall carelessly.
Finally it lost its colour.
That's how I imagine farewells,
tiny perishings in the face of time.
On this very day, it collapsed.
The stone that guarded its feet
maintains its composure.
Here begins a new era:
Year One after the Death of the Birch.

Old Man under an Apple Tree

1

Blame, always blame,
as if there weren't enough empty books
that would gladly take it on
for all eternity. Dear God, or
whoever feels responsible
for the hunger, take these apples
unto you; they belong in the light.

2

If you look down from above,
from the height of the swallows,
you can see the apples in the grass,
red like very old cherries.
The old man shakes his head
like a child whose shadow
doesn't want to obey him
on the way to sleep.

Nights on the Terrace

A bat of an eyelid
that goes unnoticed.
The Earth rolls together,
nothing more to be said
in the prophetic language.
The paper darkens
and the unfaithful letters
cannot distinguish
between Heaven and Earth.
You can still hear the world
above the closed books;
their desperate breaths,
because their words are running out.

Photo Album *

Bony lads in mouse-grey jackets,
long socks, holidays in the Harz (Auntie Annie),
crew cut, visiting Grandma (Elsie),
Saxony dialect, the first swan
on Nicholas Lake, the house opposite.
Peace on every photo, dark springs.
Thirty-four people drowned here bathing;
there was talk of a giant catfish.
Him there, with the fixed glare of a coachman;
that's Mr Rohde. He jumped out the window
because he didn't believe in the future;
what with his past. Unica Zürn.
I brought the *Revue* and a Nuremberg
stamp to Paul Scheerbart's house.
The pension had to be paid prior to death.
One more time—the house opposite.
Then a tattered photograph like a bookmark—
betray and forget. The last pages
empty; happy days, strangely empty.

Memory from School

There was one, spoke ever of acacia,
how mad she was about that scent.
She knew Pliny by heart,
Horace flowed in her veins,
Boethius was a god to her.
But when the acacias bloomed,
she could not contain herself.
Her name won't occur to me.

Class Reunion

He's now a carpenter,
he became a lawyer, she was
in the press office for public TV.
The boy I shared a desk with
does research on the brain.
He says that the opening times
of love are flexible.
How can the red
of the rosehip be described?
We're conditioned to oversee
the condition of the whole,
not the details.
Only one of us made it—
she mentioned gathering berries
in a wood in Finland
and was never seen again.

Poem

I could speak of wars,
of gods that invented life
because they were bored, of hedgehogs
in my garden, of myself.
I could speak of a man well read
in the variants of catastrophe
like a Romanian philosopher.
Laurel leaves can
cast out demons too.
But better keep your mouth shut.
The silence is loud enough.

Peripheral Symptoms of War

In dreams, all images flow
together like liquid honey.
Birds cling to air,
dripping screams at the ground
to the joy of children; and the wind
rushes in from silent lands,
to guard the unspeakable treasures of light.

A door bursts opens and mourning politely,
quietly requests material.
We are speechless and jealous of things
that have the gift of remaining silent. Look
at the way the ants count sand!
Nobody knows how long it will last
till the soldiers finally go to rest.

An officer speaks in a high-pitched voice:
From now on, you are all necessary
peripheral symptoms of war, dear citizens.
But nobody wants to admit it later.

II

'*He who kills the way*
also kills the wanderer.'

Hermann Rehse
The Language of the Baziba in German East-Africa

In the Negev

for N.C.

I have seen the bear,
the way it hugs the enemy shield
and the lion that outruns the bison
in the shadow of the tamarisk.
The hunt as knowledge you can taste.
I have counted the sand
in the Negev, the glorious sand
which cannot record my tracks.

Hotel Malibran, Venice

In the alleyway under my window,
at quarter to five in the morning,
the butcher greets the bakeress
as it was five hundred years ago,
and in the invisible sky
above me, doves laugh about
the unencrypted language.
'Everything that has its beginning
in this world
ends in this world too.'
A page is opened
in the thick book of insomnia,
and with closed eyes
I read of how the muteness of the world can be
        conquered.
Vain sentences
that celebrate the wrong 'however',
and the thinly spun 'better than nothing';
not a single gold-flooded gape of astonishment.
I want to hear the story from the beginning,

later, when we take the boat out
over the lagoon
and the water is divided as if
a downwind was angrily breaking
into a cornfield.

Hotel Near Erfurt*

Here, only the dead live,
pay with ashes.
You see their shadows
behind the windows;
shadows of children too.
The taxi driver spoke
of a mathematician
from Jena; in '45 he died;
knew the exact number of all
the dead the earth had known.
Not a single one is lost.
You can't bring luggage
if you want to move in here.
Even books are forbidden.

Message, 2012

Post from warm lands,
written in letters of ice,
clunk into the letter box.
Sender unknown.
No one should say
he did not hear the sky
screaming above the land
of the disappointed, says
the message; in future
the clouds, too, will go their
separate ways; on the lake
that mirrors our shame
lies, like homesickness,
the eternal light with which
it all began in Europe.

Hotel Europa *

Three people in a lift
trying hard not to see one another,
three incomprehensible languages
distributed over three floors,
three nights of anger.

One long, dark corridor.

At the window opposite, a woman
feeds the screams of gulls
with bread. *Mimesis*, a work
without footnotes, served as saviour.
If you rang me now,
I wouldn't understand you.

Enlightenment

Standing right here
the sea lends me
a light
that ignites me, and with my feet
I read
the Braille of pebbles.

Flight to Istanbul

The Pannonian plains, then Sofia;
hard to imagine that people live down there.
There are villages but no people.
When the Danube meets obstacles,
it just goes around them skilfully.
Sometimes there's a flash of light below;
probably a lost child
sending signals with a mirror.
That's me, I want to shout.
Tiny pillars of smoke, little-lamb clouds,
then the sea comes into view.

Harry Mulisch *

The canals are losing their water
and the boats which have been moored
since my youth are now aground.
Death is very thin in Amsterdam,
and narrow are the staircases
down which he has to stumble.
Saints step out of paintings,
their noses rusty red,
and speak Kaddish
behind hands raised in whisper.

Hotel Il Patriarca *

He slept in my room,
Federico Fellini;
in my bed,
read Jules Verne,
the man who could imagine
a future for the future.
The curtains are surely new,
but they sway, so unperturbed,
like in one of his early films.
The enemy overlooked the sign.
Fellini supposedly loved life,
so it is said, until
the cicadas drove him away
with their dumb talk.
Everything can be understood,
can be made light work of
if you love life.
Everything is light under the clouds
which are stealing away
with the next best wind.

Shame

May light. Someone came by late,
peeled himself out of the dark of the hedge
and spoke the childish language
of the branches. He looked pauperly,
his cap hanging down deep over his forehead.
He was faithful to the bats;
he praised the catechism of the animals,
but his true love was the clowning
of the butterflies before they died of cold.
We sat on the bench in front of the house
watching that wretch,
his finite swellings and fallings.
Then he continued on, the late storyteller,
leaving only his name behind,
an unspeakable name.
So many stories he had
that I could have told, I thought;
but I remained silent out of shame.

After the Rain

The river comes,
stutters towards me,
a school of violence.
It speaks through me.
No calm;
none to offer.

Before the Storm

Someone said
the wind is a tradesman
with no tools; the grass
dances, the hazelnut bushes
and the ferns collapse
as if the anger of the prophet
had got into them, and the lime,
of which was said that it praises
the great joy of the storm,
croaks tearfully.
The coming of the flood.
Hold your tongue; light-hearted words
return of their own free will;
the images of happy chambers.
Nothing is calculable.
A friend informs me:
Leopardi and Pascal died when they were 39;
and downstairs the door falls, crashing into the
    house.

Street Scene in a Foreign City

Bent over he stands
'like a question mark'
and wants to protect his shadow
which rests against the wall
darkly exhausted.
We give neither much nor little,
and between us there, sombre cars
dragging themselves through the day
like wandering camels.
The disaster cannot
be adequately described,
not even in rhyme,
because humility has flown
like smoke from the fire.
Forest people are housing in the city,
living on poison herbs
and failing as human beings.

Russian Cash

The hotel's still standing;
all the other houses
were torn down.
The pigeons are now nesting
in other city quarters.
There's no warm water, instead
a selfish light in which
only the dead can read.
We needed the money.
The young man
who carries our luggage
calls himself the manager.
It's been a long time
since he was placing invoices.

Four Lines for Lalla *

for Ranjit Hoskoté

The path that led me here
was not the path I should have taken.

If the shoes happen to lose their way,
just come barefoot to us.

Cinnamon

Suddenly someone comes up with cinnamon
as if that were the explanation
for all the secret entanglements
of heaven and earth—cinnamon.
My grandmother saved four stalks of it
through the war, no more.
The birch shakes off the winter;
the wind tests its perseverance.
And all I can think of is cinnamon.
As far as I'm concerned, you can call
the moon a pumpkin,
but when someone says cinnamon,
I can't feel anything except the warmth of the
    dead.

On Seagulls

You don't have to like seagulls,
particularly not when they're
on patrol at the beach
like grumpy waiters till
you go home finally, taciturn and tired.
But anyone who's ever seen the way
a giant American seagull,
which you could almost mistake for an albatross,
cuts the kilometre-long, thin
fabric between the sky and the water
to size, so that the earth can roll itself up
when the sun no longer warms it,
will speak of such creatures with respect.

As for what they're saying—not a word.

Countryside Cafe *

A dog passes,
reminds me of Nietzsche
the way Olde painted him,
a child's nightmare
in the dark eyes.
Read Hölderlin now,
that's safer.
In the maple, the mantra of the pigeons.
The barwoman clears the tables.
She's got a heart for sparrows.

National Museum in Calcutta

Inside dusty boxes tiny stones,
millions of years old, bones of dinosaurs,
skeletons of mice, hardly lettered,
a tortoise without a head or a neck to risk.
Its shell stands out like one of the cauldrons
in which poverty is cooked
on open fires in the streets.
It smells like a school in Berlin
when we still didn't know what the point was
of looking at bones, flints, massive needles
through which evolution threaded its hair,
without success. Here in the Museum of Calcutta
you realise that it's your own bones
hatching here in showcases. In the corner,
the fat god with the elephant's head
laughs as he speaks into his telephone—
we belong to nobody, certainly not to us.

India—Seven Postcards

1

On the scarred body
of the elephant of Jaipur
tiny birds nest.
With haste they peck
a poem into his back.
He leaves them be;
verse is good
for the skin.

2

The apes of Amber
cool their bottoms
on marble from Carrara.
A seventeenth-century gift
of the Maharajah
that he never regretted.

3

Never look the apes
who guard the relics
in the eye;
they are sworn to a god
who never forgives.

4

Before my reincarnation,
said a camel,
I was Zbigniew Herbert,
the Polish poet.
But the woman from the Goethe-Institut;
she's having none of it.
Come autumn, she's being
transferred to Prague.

5

Salman Rushdie
couldn't come;
the Muslims wanted to kill him.
Now indignant pigeons

are reading the Satanic Verses
in canon.

6

On Sunday after breakfast
sacred cows are on traffic control
in front of the Palace of Winds.
Their silence is Sanskrit.

7

In the Raj Mahal Palace Gardens
there's a wedding taking place;
the groom arrives on a horse.
A decent dowry,
two frightened eyes.
That'll have to suffice for a lifetime.
In the morning the ants collect
the leftover glitter and trinkets
before the real wedding begins.

Programme Poetry

There's nothing for it.
We'll have to describe
the thaw on the glistening
leaves of the oil tree;
the age-old hospitality
of shade, the alphabet of
the stones, uphill and downhill.
Our Achilles shield
is a dry clod of earth.
Sometimes birds fly past:
red-breasted finches,
that shorten our life.

The Hedgehog *

for Reni & Ronnie

For some days now there's been
a hedgehog
running through our garden,
long enough at least
for us to get acquainted
if we'd take the trouble to.
It must live at the neighbours' place.
There, there's a gardener
and an idle dog
that sleeps all day.
But when it's on its rounds,
then it's in our garden,
always after sunset
when its grey spines
cast no shadows.
Our closely shaven grass
signifies the end of civilization for it;
the fence a work of the devil.
Justice for the hedgehog
who knows a lot, if nothing
of the necessity of death.

How Poems Happen

Everybody knows the moment,
you step into the glade
and the rabbits,
after a second of hesitation,
vanish into the undergrowth.
There isn't any word
that could keep them there.
You've obviously lost your marbles,
said my father
when tears welled up inside me.
How can you imagine the whole
if you don't know
what the whole is?

Sleepless

A half-open door
through which the night jostles,
bringing order with it.
In the far distance, trains are passing,
each carriage the same as the next.
The travellers are sleeping, not noticing
that someone has disembarked.
He's standing at my window now,
creating a priceless vessel
of a disobedient soul.
He needs a lot of warmth.
History doesn't need me.
It stumbles on, sleepless,
with kitsch and Gloria.
But I am the vessel,
filled to the brim with doubt.
That is the lesson of the night.

Copyright

What we have experienced
belongs to history,
which feeds on us;
now it demands peace.
It's got its good suit on,
the one with the gold buttons
in which the reflection
of all that life can't
offer can be seen.
Everything we own.

III

'*Upon each hill we hoped*
to catch a glimpse of the river;
but our hopes were all in vain.'

Alfred Brehm
Travels in Sudan

Old Wooden House

The house is not suited
to hypocrisy.
It listens to itself.
The cracking walls
don't frighten it.
Only the dust
raises its voice.
The dead reside in the Village;
they accept the post.
A blind cat
acts as postman.
The man who used to
own the house
wrote a book:
The Art of
Catching a Mouse
with a Glance.
A book about everything
life can't offer.

A Poet

In his face he wears
his childhood, heavy books
close his eyes,
his hands are at rest,
inviting the shadow
to darken his bequest.

(Untitled)

A friend just announced he's coming;
he wants to stay till the end
of the year. Single-syllabic name;
his first name remains a secret.
Got a good reason probably.
A taciturn clam of a guy
who says no more, just sits the whole
day trying to talk to the dead.
Sometimes he cradles the cat
in his arm and counts her ribs.
He calls her Frieda,
otherwise incomprehensible.

In the Uckermark *

for Botho Strauß

Cobblestones treaded away at the sides;
for two hundred years the hay carts
have been trundling over them, sharing the
    harvest
with the ash trees. Hard to believe
that the Prussian corn was raised here,
where a cowherd now grazes
as if German history had never happened.
At the edge of the path lies a dead badger
enticing enthusiastic swarms of ants.
And in the valley, patient herons are watching
the fish as if it were the task of a lifetime.
Here runs our inner frontier.
Don't move. See the way the clouds divide,
drifting off to Poland.
Consult books to find out which languages
were spoken to pay tribute
to beauty and its ephemerality.
We greet the red birch, planted twenty years ago,

and which, should the lightning spare it,
will survive us, only slightly moved.

Lentils in New York

for Drenka Willen

1

Some look forward to New York
like to meeting a civilization
no traveller has yet really discovered,
there on the restless banks of the river
and on the streets where cash is paid
with monomaniacal fanaticism, before
    disappearing
into the shadow of greed for ever.
They are looking forward to New York
because here they can feel their dependence
on people they've never met in their lives.
Just imagine a city in which only the dead
live, deeply involved in correspondence
because they want to have a past
at all costs. The dead live on
out of spite. They sit in black limousines
that dream, like giant old cats,
of saving the silence that was once native to here.

2

As for me, when I think of New York
I see the plate of lentils in front of me,
that's waiting for me in the Village
in a red brick house. Like the foolish Esau
who sold his birthright for a plate of lentils
to Jacob, I would hand the city over
for a plate of Drenka's thousand lentils,
Serbian fruit, polished Orthodox, five thousand
      years long.

Almost Nothing

I dreamt of a tiny torch
which cast a shadow searching for help.
The shadow was always behind me,
always there, where there was still hope
of understanding the darkness.
Was I walking before me or following myself?
I came to a place in which tears
were being counted; seven tears for a lost world.
That's how I found my way back; the door
    sprang open
and I saw, where the books had once stood,
a thriving world.

Lost Time

The taxi comes too late, the bus
can't wait for you and, for technical
reasons, the plane refuses
to leave solid ground. You know
how that is, the hollow stomach,
deep, hard and dark,
lost time. Public telephones—
that was yesterday. And I wouldn't have
known how to explain it.
So many words people say
just to get rid of them. Spit it out!
Foreign taxis and buses squirming before you;
above you, aeroplanes cross, their veils
drifting off to the destination at which
your anecdote was meant to be received.
Half of heaven is burning.
A beginning without a beginning,
an end without an end and a lightning bolt
that tears up time like old paper.

Written From the Heart

Maybe it's really true
that no other task was ever given to us
than to swap some words around
on the page, so that the short text
that accounts for our life can be read another way
and creates other images than
the ones inside us, piled up and
torn at the edges—and yet
as clear as had they been dreamt.
On top there's one with nothing but sky on it.
It's called: departure vanishing.

Istanbul Revisited *

for Sezer Duru

Thirty years later I visited the carps
in the cisterns of Istanbul once more.
There was a ship burning in Bosporus
at that time, an oil tanker christened
with the name *Independenta*.
Like a rusty turtle it was snapping
for air to fire up the flames,
and young Anatolian soldiers
were forced to use quick-fire machine guns
to drive off the smoke that hung black
over the city and left us speechless.
I can still see the thick knots of cables
on streets mottled with crows,
working on contract with the secret services,
tapping the whispers for mutton prices,
love and work in Germany.
From Afrasyab's towers, the owl announced the hour
and the spiders wove the curtains in the palace of
    the Caesars.

Then I saw the carps again in the cistern
of Istanbul. Since Justinian's time, they've been
    informants
for the state and fate of the empire.
With the passion of heavy animals, they cover
the mossy stones with gloom;
my age-old brothers who know everything
and undertake nothing, do not even glance upwards
when they're hit by a coin from Europe.
Some of them lie miserable and dark like marquetry
on the ground, dabble and read in
the *Historia Arcana* of the barbarian invasion.
It's the lack of light that saves them.

Old Well

It's all about these groundwater crustaceans,
tiny animals with spikes and bristles
that have their habitat in the limnic
    mesopsammon—
the scree of pebbles and sand found on banks.
They came from Australia, reaching
Madagascar in Jura and were seen
long before the South Atlantic emerged,
in America, by groundwater mites,
for example. Scolopidic or scuttelar bristles;
they all make up a family of sixty species
in nineteen genera and speak Latin.
Nature wouldn't have reckoned
with their existence quite yet.
If you happen to be grubbing around
in the mud of old wells after sunset and come
by chance across Parabathynellidae, treat them
with respect; they are older than you.

Diel *

His own butter pear
is accredited to him,
as well as the Liveland Raspberry Apple
the form and taste of which
he described more exactly
than the art historians
illuminated the fruit in Dutch paintings.
Colour and texture of the flesh,
location and culture of the ground;
the Great English Rennet
simply would not leave him be.
Researched through and through,
and the system of the fruit trees
had no Homer until he came.
My apple tree
bears fruit once more, and all of them
are inedible and beautiful.

Walking, Slightly Moved *

for Karl Anton Rickenbacher

A long, erratic river,
uncertainly drawn ink,
tired of sounds and drained,
and light steps,
true to the old words.
The trees, the survivors,
are mirrored in the dark water
that gathers in the sea.
What can one then write
to evade life?
In the monastery, under the lime,
salvation is buzzing, the bees
celebrate consent to the world.
Even the sun misses its goal
of enlightening the melancholy.

Czesław Miłosz *

The year had begun so well.
I was allowed to visit St Roch
who healed the animals whilst, at the other side
of the street, revolutions were breaking out
and ejecting their blood onto screens.
The tiny door of memory,
so long closed, opened suddenly
and I saw myself, in the middle of Venice,
sitting on a bench that was reserved
for death. Women passed me by
whispering secret messages
on the way to the station or the boat.
Then Miłosz came towards me,
the walking stick in his back, a net
of glittering fish in his hand.
He didn't look very dead at all,
standing there reciting poetry,
the same way others talk about rising prices
for truth, for fruit and vegetables.

Translating

My neighbour translates
Persian poetry,
ghazals, as if it hadn't all
been said already.
Sometimes I hear him
screaming, liberated
by the metre,
in search of a German word
for God.

Once he's finished,
he calls.
He wants to hear, not read.
What might, he asks,
have happened, in
the 'seven cities of love'?
He doesn't want to know
about censorship.

God wrote too much.
With that, he hangs up.

Outdated

It's calming to leaf through old books
that are long outdated. Novalis, Hamann, just
    casually,
without any deeper intention. When ink still existed.
When people still wanted something of life. On the
    radio
Mahler is playing to raise the roof.
There's a carpet of light spread out on the grass.
The entirety of human culture, says a Frenchman,
could fit into a single hand. I listen to the crickets;
they appreciate Mahler. An eternal recurrence
in another form,
incomprehensible yet totally clear.

What Still Has to be Done! *

for Peter Handke on his 70th birthday

Collect the nuts
before the squirrel gets them;
bring the shadows to safety;
talk to the pencil
when it holds back with words;
refuse to find the enemy
hatching in unthought thoughts;
read the clouds,
the perpetual epic
on form and metamorphosis;
lift the stone from the brow;
give a last deadline to astonishment.

And don't forget to look for the place
where the book is hiding,
the book with the empty pages,
the empty book, the book.

Antonio Tabucchi is Dead *

The night sky is now so close
that you can see the chaff of light moths
mediate between the stars.
Three wishes granted to disentangle
the confusion of being, the joyful science
of failure. The sea can be heard;
it will be here soon, the wind
carries it beyond desire.
Three wishes? Everything waits, till finally
someone snuffs out the candle before the morning.

Literarisches Colloquium, Berlin*

He still knows me, the old fox; grey
and blind he is now. He can see
with his ears. It was the '50s when we
got to know each other, just after
Stalin's death, in the sunny gardens,
studying the didactic play of fear
which was meant for the just and the unjust.
We took a boat to Kleist's grave;
you could hear the shots better from there,
when somebody gathering mushrooms
touched the invisible wire.
In winter you could hear the local trains screech.
In summer we only heard ourselves.
My school was across the tracks,
where love was taught, and Latin.
What was the name of the music teacher
who jumped out of the window?
I was already here before I was allowed
to write my name with a pencil
in handwriting that no longer knows me.

Doesn't want to know any more.
The fox makes a pause, grey and blind.

Nicolas Born *

I'd very much like to see Born again,
who slept here,
in this bed, in this hotel,
shortly before it was renovated.
Gerald Bisinger, the poet,
worked as a room waiter then,
and brought fresh beer.
We talked about things
that hadn't been,
that never will have been.
Ach, the sad riches
of his high, light song.
The spider was already there then,
weaving a web for me
in which I could suffocate, almost.

Claude Simon *

Claude Simon sat
beside me in the dream,
green in the face.
He'd eaten meatballs
by mistake,
in Wannsee in Berlin.
I pulled him back
into real life by
his little hands.
We drank his wine,
a provincial red,
and read the Georgics
which he wanted to rewrite
after the war.
'Forget self-realization',
was really all he said.
Talking wasn't his strong point.
'See that butterfly?'
He said before going,
Odysseus doesn't want to go home.'
At that, I woke up.

A Reminder*

for Zev Birger

I hear the freight trains
that drive through your life.
Between the sleepers
I hear your voice which
does not yet know
how much we will remember it.
The voice of a traveller
who crossed a desert,
a desert of ground bones
that we thought was sand,
before we got to know you.

Whodunnit?

In last year's honey, suspended,
wholly untouched,
a fly.
The perfect murder.
The way a crime novel
might begin
or end.

Mirror

It takes a hopelessly long time
to get a rough idea of who you are.
The ineffaceable love of apple trees,
the history written in the clouds.
Research on grass, not intended
for printing, enchanted water,
rendezvous in the accessible darkness.
Nothing for gods, really.
Breathe to escape the curse;
hopelessly long, yet so short.
Too short.

Tidying Up

The books
that don't fit into the alphabet.
The pictures
overloading my head.
The words
that flatter the sea.
The escape routes
that lead right back.
The childish love
for crows.

Like when I watched
a dog dying.
The tent city of mushrooms.
The protocols of humility.
A thousand types
of infinity.

No longer wanting
to know everything.

Will what we
always knew
now come?
In free verse
or in rhyme?

The solidarity
with the stones
and a sponge
for happy words.

In the Shed

A rake that's missing three prongs,
a rusty scythe, unsharpened,
a book to study the grasses,
dog-eared by sun and rain,
mousetraps, broken slates;
memories, not very talkative.
Sometimes they rise and
scatter themselves around the terrain;
but most of them remain seated,
as if they were no longer part of me.

IV

*'It was the year in which they
dissolved the Ministry for Weather.'*

Aleš Šteger

The Book of Bodies *

Snow

It smells like snow,
a smell that needs no description,
no great words of admiration.
The last waves are twitching over the sea,
pencil thin, until the ice
prints them in regular verses.

We live well,
read papers, watch TV and see
the ways of Hamlet's doubts;
we love Mörike and Schubert's improvisations
and poverty's not something we shrug shoulders at,
neither when it's near nor when it's distant.

Our neighbour knew everything about Sanskrit,
just took his own life
because his wife left him. Right now
we just saw him in the garden with the blackbirds,
crooked as a question mark, birds
like hopping dots around him.

We live longer than intended,
distinguish right terms
from wrong ones. We love the snow
when the pathways are like the borders
of obituaries. With long, wide tracks,
death runs from life,

vanishes quickly into the white.

Short Trip

Still evening, got the bike
out of the shed,
rode down to the river
following the trail of the wind.
Midges were underway
and occasionally people.
It can't really be said
whether the world is vanishing
without any witnesses
around to confirm it.
You hear the birches laughing,
when the insects get
too close to them, otherwise
hardly anything at all.
I don't know where
the trail leads. I look
into the sad riches
of green and continue on
into what's never been
but will have been
before darkness falls.

Summerhouse at Easter

A drift of leaves before the house.
Last year's threats, bursting out
of the letter box and old newspapers,
count their own dead;
those of the others don't count, at least,
unless it was we who killed them.
We? Yes—we. Four months later
we can happily play with the plural.
There's a dead jay on the terrace.
Last summer he was my friend.
The trees still bare. Through the branches
I can see the lake; a ship, dead tired,
being hugged by water.
No one knows how beauty comes to be
and nobody wants to know why
we need it—so that, just for once,
we don't have to talk about it.
We. We have no other choice.

The Current State of Affairs, 2012

So, that's supposed to be summer.
I open the window to hear the rain,
the way it drums on the shed,
its hissing scribble on the grass.
I watch the sparrows which,
since their birth, have known no more
than these thin, glass strips
that strike the ground and dissipate.
If I count the sum of all the shadows,
it will soon become a darkness which
could encourage a dreamy utopist, even,
to open their heart once more to eternity.
You have to turn the light on
to be able to imagine a future.
Or you just paint landscapes
with ruins in which sheep live.
And goats that don't care
whether they chose this place or
it was allocated to them.

At the Lake

An age-old land, distinguished by moraine.
When the sun or the lightning lights it up,
it fades and becomes unrecognizable.
You don't know if you belong to it;
like the tree trunk in the dying waves,
rolling as if it had no future,
you bear your life like everything else.
On the other side of the lake, a last hayfield
before the winter; the rain has pulled
the thin grass out of the field once more.
The trees are bare already; crows replace
the leaves of the lime tree. There is, so they say,
another way of reading autumn,
told by the water in a helpless dialect.

Near Boston, at the Sea

The wind, tired of the thorny hedges,
has finally stopped—
now, please be calm, too, dear sea!
The morning like cold ashes.
Even the insects do without
their heathen craftsmanship.
Breathing seems like
an invention with which
we seek familiarity.
Can't see much of God
in this light.

Expecting Rain

The grass has got to be cut;
it's grown too long. Planes lock
the sky with
pale writing, seeing everything—
the house, the grass, me.
We're being recorded as if
it all depended on us. What then happens
everyone knows; we're the past of
the future. Of the grass
remains just a tale that explains it all
but can't be read.
God roars. It's going to rain.

Autumn

The sun has burrowed itself into the wood
of the hay barn to warm my back for me
for the last time in this year, probably.
The wood speaks incessantly at the first hint
of an approaching bee or one of those beetles
which crash against the planks, plump and carefree;
it's almost as if they wanted to put an end to the
     wooden prattle.
Further down the slope, the wasps have
burrowed into the meadow to found a city,
a city without light, and everything must make way
     for it;
they have even driven the mole away.
The sun is now leaving the ninth house;
the lime is in her way; its last leaves
are moving with the eastern wind, as if
the sky was breathing out to free itself.
I was sometimes gazed upon by others, a spared one
allowed to spread his dreams out
when we, already in the shade, on the shady side,

talked about what we are and what we
want to be. Now the world has long
moved on and I'm still here, sitting,
my back to the wood, in my hand
a rolled-up leaf that's trying to hide its beauty.

At the Baltic Sea, Very Early

1

Restless as the pitter-patter steps of
sand lizards, looking for yesterday's tracks
in the morning.
Like stalks of grass that cast no shadows.

Children, tired from sleep,
growl at the sea.

It took a long time
for the Kaiser's message
to finally be washed ashore.
But nobody wants to hear it now.

2

Empty snail shells. Mussels.
The good always seems better than it is,
evil, as always, too talkative.

Chiusi, Terre di Siena

A bilingual vase before my eyes,
apparently Etruscan, thus, very old.
Mustiola drank from it,
the martyr who is known to everybody,
though no one has ever seen her.
Now she belongs to me too.
If someone should remember me,
they will not know
what connected me to this vase.

The Spider and I

Look at the way the spider
forfeits its life
strand for strand,
an age-old craft,
purest art.
I find notes
in my books,
in my writing,
written by spiders—
Orpheus among the animals.
Yet another reprieve
for the spider and me
and the last strand
that dare not snap.

The Blackbird

The wind which, now restlessly,
captivates the apple trees and plunders them,
as if the harvest had to be in by evening,
steals form and posture from
the blackbird which is trying hard
to sing me free of the storm.
I see, from behind the window, the way
it races, despite its upright wings, towards me.
The pane shivers lightly under the impact;
the bird falls. What can I do?
Its shroud, the black one that I've known
since it first stormed out of the hedges
towards me, is now stained.
Even the paper, on which I'd intended
to clarify who I am, has now blackened,
lies before me in rigor mortis;
won't do service to a love song.

Early Sun in the South

On the walls, lizards
hang like trophies.
Light gathers, snuffs
the handwriting out
in which the good news
was written.
You see the buzzard?
It wrote its share:
The ashes are still warm.

Cutting Grass

Tearing through the grass with
a blunt scythe, touching riches and
greatness only in passing.
Every straw that will not bow
is a microphone with which the dead
remain in touch, confess what they've
neglected as if an end were nigh.
You have to pull, not push, the blade
in time with the rattling heart.
Cows are down in the valley, indecisive, standing
with heavy udders on their meadow.
And a bird cries out
as if there were some
good news to spread that had been spared us
up to now. Any chance there was
of taking leave is growing less; that's why the grass
has to suffer—the carefree grass—
this cut will not be repeated.

End of the Summer

I watch the moths, the way
they crash against the glass,
a noise like shattering ice.
The bitter censorships
—for which we curse the summer,
stealing away—
taking the birds with them.
Mealy nuts
and the smell of old hay,
as if there was nothing more
to expect than that.
The house quakes and the table
tells a dark story,
brought from another life
that remains unknown to us.

Reverie

Sunk in thoughts of itself, a wind
sits in the trees at my window
defying the babbling mourning
rain. Everything stops at once,
even the prospective Arma-
geddons and the breeding of stupidity.
How tiny the titmice are! And
how well they interrogate trees.
It would, of course, doubtless, be wrong
to rely on reason now;
it contains nothing
that could feed our dreams.

Still Pool

A still pool
in the wood, touched
now and again by insects.
A thick surface
of seeds and leaves
refusing to heed the lift of the wind.
At night, large animals
drink here, though only
at night; so that we
won't be embarrassed by any need
to find another word
for still pool.

Clearing

1

The drama of the leaves
when they fall; and you,
from afar, try to understand
a world in which nobody knows
any more what farewell means,
retreating halfway
between the eye and the heart.

2

Leaves mourn the dead;
only sparrows, untroubled,
succumb to the bribery of crumbs.
The coming world,
seen through an evil eye,
makes a start
in the helpful heart of the words.

3

Everything trembles.
And God trembles too.

Notes

p. 5, 'Postcard, May 2012'

The poet was born in the 'wartime' year of 1943.

p. 8, 'Near Münsing'

Münsing is a village near Munich.

p. 11, 'I Cannot Divine What it Meaneth'

The title is from the first line of Mark Twain's translation of Heinrich Heine's 'Die Lorelei' ('The Loreley', 1880).

p. 12, 'Wooden House'

Alfred Kolleritsch (b. 1931) is an Austrian writer, poet and philosopher particularly known for his opposition to the 'return of the never-changing'—to a society plagued by narrowness and stagnation. As founder of the Austrian literature magazine *Manuskripte*, he has aided many lesser-known writers to greater success.

p. 24, 'Photo Album'

Mr Rohde was the poet's music teacher at school.

Unica Zürn (1916–70) was a German author and painter particularly remembered for her anagram poetry and her automatic drawings. She was also the partner of the German artist and author, Hans Bellmer.

The *Revue* is a German glossy magazine. As a child, the poet was a paper boy.

The Nuremberg stamp was the insurance stamp of the Nuremberg Life Assurance company.

Paul Scheerbart (1863–1915) was a German author of fantastic literature and drawings and one of the few German writers who was outspokenly against the First World War.

p. 34, 'Hotel Near Erfurt'

Erfurt is a town in East Germany.

p. 36, 'Hotel Europa'

This poem was written in Istanbul.

Mimesis (1953) by the German emigrant Erich Auerbach (1892–1957) was written in Istanbul without access to a library and with very few footnotes.

p. 39, 'Harry Mulisch'

Harry Mulisch (1927–2010) was a Dutch writer. Mulisch's mother was a German Jew while his Dutch father was a Nazi collaborator. His life and literary work were greatly influenced by the Nazi era and the Shoah.

p. 40, 'Hotel Il Patriarca'

Federico Fellini (1920–93) was an Italian film director and scriptwriter. Fellini actively evaded categorization of his work, strictly going his own way. A quote from one of his interviews, 'Fellini is creating Fellini again', could be said to describe the personal individualism of his work.

Jules Verne (1828–1905) was a French writer renowned for his adventure novels.

p. 46, 'Four Lines for Lalla'

Ranjit Hoskoté (b. 1969) is an Indian poet, cultural theorist and curator of exhibitions. He is also a journalist for the English-language newspaper The *Hindu* in Bombay.

p. 49, 'Countryside Cafe'

Hans Olde (1855–1917) was a German painter. His 1899 portrait of the mentally ill Friedrich Nietzsche, who died soon after it was made, is extremely well-known.

p. 55, 'The Hedgehog'

Ronald M. Dworkin (1931–2013) was an American philosopher and author of *Justice for Hedgehogs* (2011).

p. 64, 'In the Uckermark'

Botho Strauß (b. 1944) is a German writer and playwright whose plays list among the most performed works on German stages.

p. 71, 'Istanbul Revisited'

Sezer Duru (b. 1942) is a Turkish translator who has translated authors such as Max Frisch, Heinrich Böll and Hans Magnus Enzensberger.

p. 74, 'Diel'

August Diel (1756–1839), founder of Pomology and author of *Attempt at a Systematic Description of Existing Types of Fruit in Germany*.

p. 75, 'Walking, Slightly Moved'

Karl Anton Rickenbacher (b. 1940) is a Swiss conductor who has worked in several places including the Zurich Opera and the BBC Scottish Symphony Opera.

p. 76, Czesław Miłosz

Czesław Miłosz (1911–2004) was a Polish writer and translator of Lithuanian origin. He was awarded the Nobel Prize for literature in 1980.

p. 79, 'What Still Has to be Done!'

Peter Handke (b. 1942) is a renowned Austrian novelist and playwright.

p. 80, 'Antonio Tabucchi is Dead'

Antonio Tabucchi (1943–2012) was an Italian writer honoured with several prestigious Italian literature prizes. He was also a translator known particularly for the Italian edition of Fernando Pessoa's works.

p. 81, 'Literarisches Colloquium, Berlin'

The Literarisches Colloquium, Berlin is a house of literature at Wannsee Lake, Berlin. It is well-known as a venue for writers and as a place of literary discussion.

Heinrich von Kleist (1777–1811) was a classic German writer, well-known for his novellas. He committed suicide at Wannsee Lake.

p. 83, 'Nicolas Born'

Nicolas Born (1937–79) was a German novelist and poet, influenced by the American Beat generation. He was socially active and an opponent of atomic power up to his death at the age of 42.

Gerald Bisinger (1936–99) was an Austrian poet who worked at the Literarisches Colloquium.

p. 84, 'Claude Simon'

Claude Simon (1913–2005) was a French novelist and the 1985 Nobel Laureate for Literature.

p. 85, 'A Reminder'

Zev Birger (1929–2011) was a Lithuanian Jew who was director of the Jerusalem Book Fair for many years.

p. 91, 'It was the year in which they / dissolved the Ministry for Weather.'

Aleš Šteger (b. 1973) is a Slovenian poet and translator. His collection of poetry *Knjiga teles* (*The Book of Bodies*) was published in 2010.

p. 95, 'New Year, 2012'

Molybdomancy is a tradition at New Year in Germany and other northern European countries, where little blocks of lead are melted and poured into cold water. The resulting cast gives insight into the coming year.

New Year, 2012 *

1

Snowflakes falling,
from down below upwards.
I hear steps
looking for a disaster,
some unreadable catastrophe,
pouring lead castings,
spilling blood.
No one remembers why
we've become the way we are.
But here we are, still here.
We just lost sight
of each other a moment.

2

Above the tree line,
the last of the stone pines,
gagged by the storm.
In summer, the shepherd was here
beside it, trying his best

to get along without history,
without beginning or end.
The sheep thanked him for it.

3

Who can imagine
what would have become of us?

New Year

Strange words are doing their rounds
and nobody understands them. Where's the
      teacher?
He's working on an inaccessible work;
the truth, that inflammable stuff;
it has to be opened up. Europe awakens;
the dark space between the heavens and the earth
is filling up with greed. Last year
we were still discussing clouds
that wanted to comfort the sand,
the rebellious sand. Slowly
the new year is moving into gear.
There's one who'd love to have a peach right now,
and everybody looks, bewildered, at him.

Winter

We want to get noticed,
but we don't get noticed.
What we occasionally notice
is strange movements
that remind us of some esoteric cult
at one with the world.
The anglers are frozen and
under the ice, on the hook,
a fish is squirming.

Wretched Apples in February

And still apples hang on the bare branches,
spared by the frost as it came
from the south overnight
with a raw bite and sealed shut the land,
the garden and the view into the garden
and the heart, too, that dreamed up the snow.
And what apples! Skin split open
and brown, nibbled flesh;
not even the blackbirds will touch them.
Dreadful, sad—as if the war
that was announced for spring
had already torn through.
I stood and looked until I saw nothing else
that bore comparison to these wretched apples.

Snow Dreamer

On the other side of the lake
I see people. They're moving,
pushing something before them
through the snow, as in life,
and seem to be enjoying it there
in the company of the wind.
Then the thaw sets in.
Everything that isn't becomes visible
Everything becomes visible; to be heard is
nothing.

Dreamings

A late afternoon
that I spent in the grass
among the birds.
I thought up a past
for the grasshopper and
a story for the ant.
I wanted to ask forgiveness of
the tiniest animals.
In the evening I was so small
myself that death
missed me on his rounds
with his bloody nuisances.
The trees bunched together.
Like uncut books, they looked
like a cemetery for all
the animals that died today.

Palm Sunday, 2012

When the sea awakens,
the silence glows. At a great height,
just under a pale moon,
the seagulls draw an image of man
as we would have it.
They show us how community is created
and disintegrates, an art
addressed to us. We watch.
Out of the grass of the beach the sun
rises; it shows the tiny birds
the way to the sea. God becomes
a pebble under the stormy waves.
He tells the story of the end
that will never end—as long as the gulls
don't touch the earth.

Corbara, 1 April

Seedlings

Today, our two agaves
were brought back, having spent winter
at full bed and board, in a nursery
around the corner, in a greenhouse,
together with more distinguished plants,
such as are held in esteem in our quarter.
I thought they would have slept
and dreamt of Mexico or the Levant,
of tired mules and of the silence,
after the bombs strike.
Rather, quite the opposite—
more than twenty seedlings peeking out
from underneath their gherkin-green sabres,
carefree and curious like young kittens.
Cut them off? asks the gardener
who smells of damp wool.
They'll either break the clay pot
or die together.
I'm sixty-eight years old now,
I can't decide.
Come end of October, we'll know more.

Beach Cafe

The cafe is still open;
the dead are sitting there
on chained-up chairs, drinking wine
on our costs. There's a few houses—
fished out of the sea—watching.
A beggar collects coins and
throws them to the dead as a sacrifice.
From the bar, stretching down to the sea,
there's a narrow strip of light
on which the dead retreat,
over the water. We remain, sitting there,
until the day rubs its eyes.